FROM COTTON TO T-SHIRTS

by Cari Meister • Illustrated by Albert Pinilla

AMICUS ILLUSTRATED and AMICUS INK are published by Amicus
P.O. Box 1329, Mankato, MN 56002
www.amicuspublishing.us

LIBRARY OF CONGRESS CATALOGING-IN-PUBLICATION DATA
Names: Meister, Cari, author.
Title: From cotton to t-shirts / by Cari Meister; illustrations by Albert Pinilla.
Description: Mankato, Minnesota : Amicus Illustrated - Amicus Ink, [2020] | Series: Who made my stuff?
Identifiers: LCCN 2018035498 (print) | LCCN 2018039619 (ebook) | ISBN 9781681517766 (pdf) | ISBN 9781681516943 (library binding) | ISBN 9781681524801 (pbk.)
Subjects: LCSH: T-shirts—Juvenile literature. | Cotton manufacture—Juvenile literature.
Classification: LCC TT675 (ebook) | LCC TT675 .M45 2020 (print) | DDC 677/.0286—dc23
LC record available at https://lccn.loc.gov/2018035498

EDITOR: Wendy Dieker
DESIGNER: Kathleen Petelinsek

Printed in the United States of America
HC 10 9 8 7 6 5 4 3 2 1
PB 10 9 8 7 6 5 4 3 2 1

ABOUT THE AUTHOR

Cari Meister has written more than 200 books for children, including the TINY series (Viking), and the FAIRY HILL series (Scholastic). She lives in Vail, Colorado with her husband and four sons, where the T-shirt is the most preferred clothing choice. Cari loves to visit schools and libraries. Find out more at carimeister.com

ABOUT THE ILLUSTRATOR

Albert Pinilla is a freelance illustrator based between Barcelona and Finland. He has worked for many publishers and companies across Europe, Asia, and the United States. He's always looking forward to new and exciting projects. To see his work, visit www.albertpinilla.com

You want a new T-shirt? Cotton T-shirts are the most popular piece of clothing in the world. But what if you had to make the T-shirt from scratch? You would need to grow the cotton, turn it into cloth at a factory, and then sew the fabric into a shirt.

Do you want to see how it's done? Great! First stop: a Texas cotton field. Texas is the perfect environment for growing cotton. It's warm and dry with plenty of sunshine.

You're in luck. See the pink flowers? They only appear for a day or two. Tomorrow, they will wither and fall off.

Small, hard bolls form where the flowers were. A boll looks a little like leaves curled into a ball. Over the next few months, the bolls grow. Then—

Pop! They burst open, revealing a fluffy white fiber. The cotton bolls are now ready for harvest.

VRROOOM! Watch out for the picker. It moves quickly row by row. It pulls the fluffy cotton boll from the plant. The picker also separates the boll from most of the stems and leaves. The cotton is then dumped into a boll buggy.

Look over there. Do you see the big pile of cotton? The cotton is pressed together into a mattress shape the size of a semi-truck trailer.

HONK! HONK! A truck comes. A belt in the trailer pulls the pile of cotton into the back of the truck. Jump in! This truck is heading to the cotton gin factory.

At the factory, the gin removes the rest of the sticks and dirt. This machine also separates the white cotton fiber from the cottonseeds. Seeds are saved to make cottonseed oil.

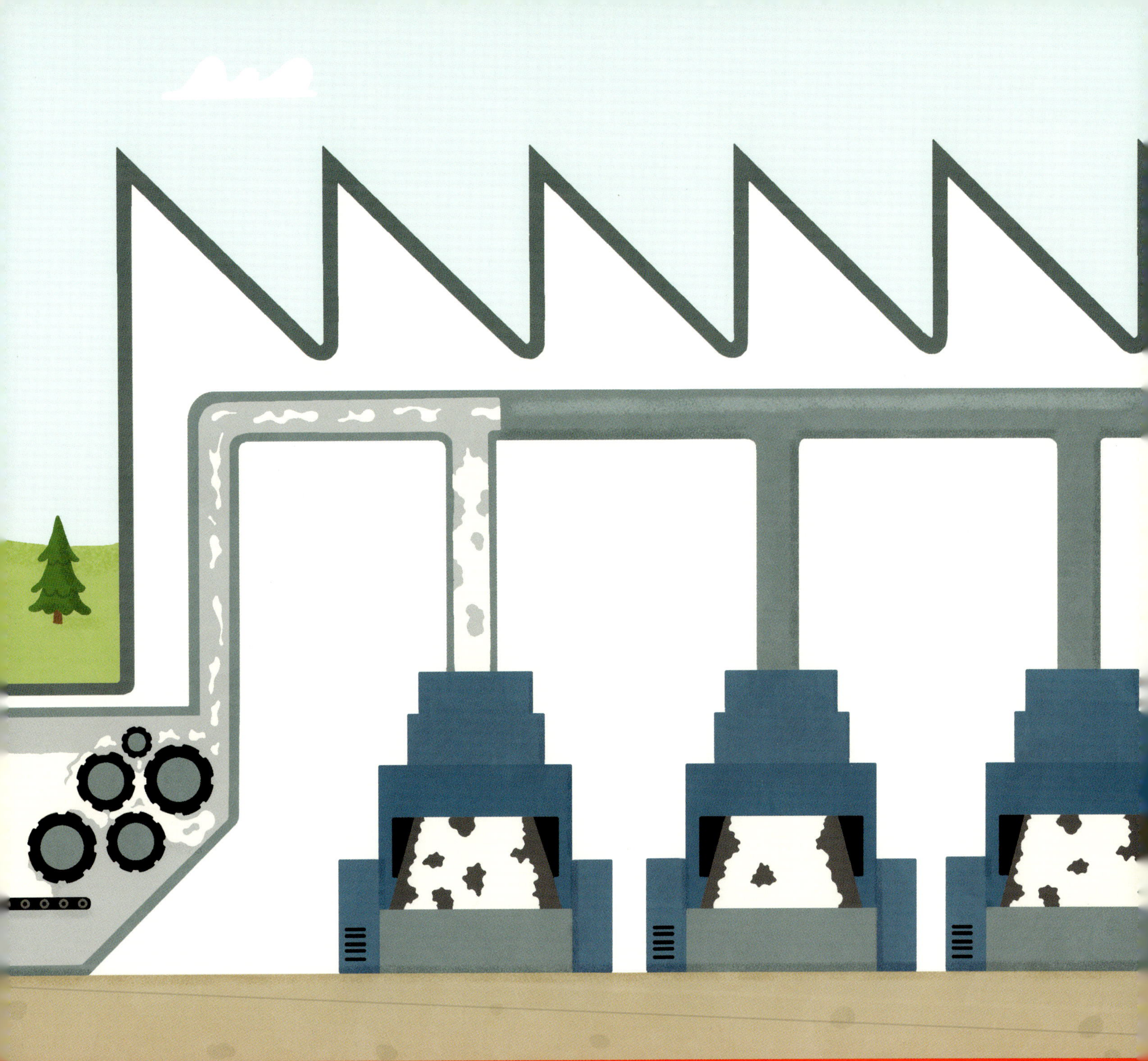

The clean, dry cotton is then bundled into bales. Another truck takes the bales to the coast where they are loaded onto a ship. Do you have your passport? This cotton is going to a factory in China.

At the spinning factory, the bales are separated and blended back together. This makes a more uniform blend of fibers. Big machines comb the fibers into long strands.

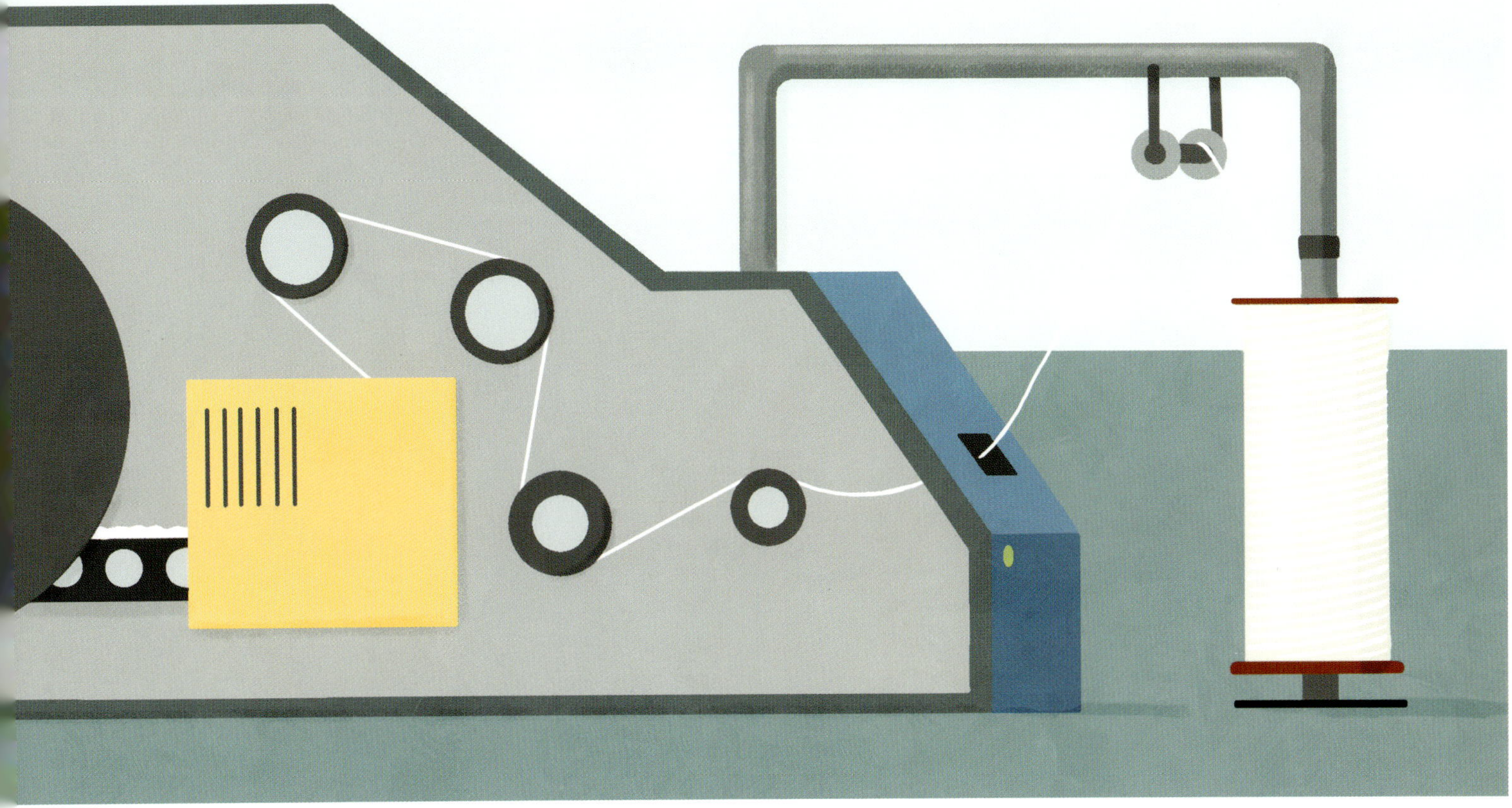

The strands are pulled and twisted together to make yarn. The yarn for T-shirts is pulled into very thin threads. Machines wind the thin yarn onto big spools.

Now the yarn is sent to a mill. Here, knitting machines weave the yarn into sheets of fabric. Some fabric is dipped into bleach to make it bright white. Other fabric is dipped into dye to color it.

It's time to make shirts! A cutter cuts the cotton fabric. Another worker sews the pieces together.

The finished shirts are packed into boxes and shipped to stores around the world.

Phew! That was a lot of steps. But thanks to the cotton farmer, the factory workers, and the T-shirt manufacturers, you can now buy a T-shirt in a store. Which one will you pick?

MAPPING MANUFACTURING

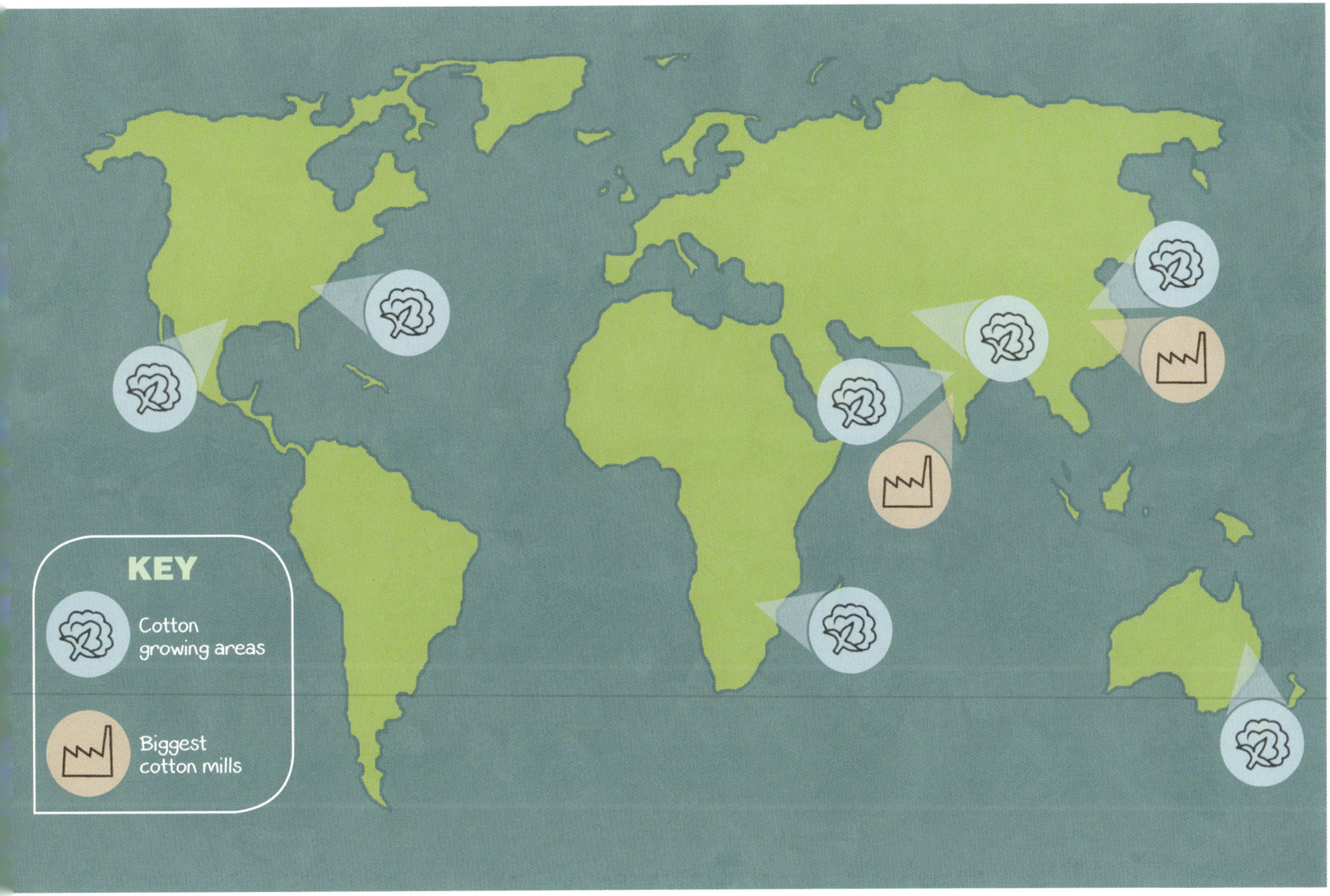

GLOSSARY

bleach A chemical that takes color away from fabric, making the fabric white.

boll The fruit of a cotton plant where the seeds are produced; this is where the fluffy cotton comes from.

cotton gin A machine used to separate fluffy cotton lint from cottonseeds.

dye A substance used to add color to fabric.

fiber The fluffy white threads inside a cotton boll.

harvest The gathering of crops that are used for food or other products.

mill A factory where cotton fibers are turned into yarn and bolts of fabric.

WEBSITES

16 Facts About Cotton
https://www.barnhardtcotton.net/blog/16-facts-about-cotton-that-you-dont-know/
Learn some facts about cotton plants and fabrics.

A Journey of Cotton, from Field to Fabric
http://www.ldc.com/blog/in-field/journey-cotton-field-fabric/
Watch as a cotton plant grows, ripens, and is processed into fabric.

Cotton Facts for Kids
https://kids.kiddle.co/Cotton
Read about how cotton is harvested and milled into several fabric products.

Every effort has been made to ensure that these websites are appropriate for children. However, because of the nature of the Internet, it is impossible to guarantee that these sites will remain active indefinitely or that their contents will not be altered.

READ MORE

Butterworth, Christine. **Where Did My Clothes Come From?** Somerville, Mass.: Candlewick, 2015.

Hayes, Amy. **Turning Cotton into Clothes**. New York: Cavendish Square Publishing, 2016.

Rivera, Andrea. **Cloth**. Mankato, Minn.: Abdo, 2017.